Arun Jeetoo

*I Want to Be the One
You Think About at Night*

First published in 2020
by Waterloo Press (Hove)
95 Wick Hall
Furze Hill
Hove BN3 1NG
Printed in Palatino 10pt by
One Digital
54 Hollingdean Road
East Sussex BN2 4AA

© Arun Jeetoo 2020

All rights remain with the author.

Cover image: © 'Couple in love holding each other under starry sky mountains and moon on seaside' by Lina Kadrova.

Author photograph © Daniel Lawton 2020

Arun Jeetoo is hereby identified as author of this work in accordance with Section 77 of the Copyright,
Designs and Patents Act 1988

This book is sold subject to the condition that it shall not, by way of trade or otherwise, be lent, resold, hired out or otherwise circulated without the author's prior consent in any form of binding or cover other than that in which it is published and without a similar condition including this condition being imposed on the subsequent purchaser.

A CIP record for this book is available from the British Library

ISBN: 978-1-906742-92-8

Acknowledgments

First and foremost, I would like to thank the Creative Writing department at Roehampton University, specifically Jeff Hilson. In the process of putting this pamphlet together I realized how far I have come—from a shy, inexperienced poet who did not take his work seriously, to a confident poet dedicated to developing my craft. You have given me the power, skills, and platform to believe in my passion and pursue my dreams. I could never have done this without the faith you have in me.

To my mother, Sandie Jeetoo. You are my #1 fan I am eternally grateful for your wisdom and support in the process of putting this pamphlet together from start to finish. Although I did not always take your advice lightly, and thought you were wrong or ill-judged most of the time, I had faith that you know best because you are my mother.

Most importantly, my never-ending appreciation and thank-yous go to the Waterloo Press team who made my dreams come true of publishing a poetry pamphlet, but also eased me into this mad world of writing and publishing poetry with so much guidance, faith and laughter. You all inspire me every day to keep up writing poetry and change the world whatever way I can.

To my editor, Naomi Foyle. You are much more than an editor to me—a mentor and friend. A compassionate, kind, intelligent human being, who taught me well on how to edit a manuscript for content and style. There could never be any words that truly express my gratitude for you.

Dedicated to:

My cat Buster, for all the long nights and early mornings editing my manuscript by my side—even though you sat by me because you wanted to be fed.

My sister Natasha, for always reading my manuscript and being too polite to offer constructive criticism. That is a real #2 fan.

My father, who is not an avid fan of poetry, but always finds ways to support me in my writing wherever he can.

The rest of my family and friends, who have put up with my nonconformist nature, nonstop creativity and sheer genius for way too long—you can now rest as the world will experience this too.

Contents

Bounty	1
Summer	2
70 Days	4
Alexa, Do You Love Me?	6
Let Me Be	7
'Did you say *Yes*?' Said He	9
Sweet	10
Summer Tree	11
Cinderella's Brother	12
They	13
Sunflower	14
Autumn eyes	16
My Jumper	17
Elbow Kiss	19
I haunt your brain with my funeral	20
Since That Night	21
Flatmate	22
Jitters	23
Let It Go	24
I Want to Be the One You Think About At Night	25

Bounty

Love is a bullet that penetrates your plastic skin.
Punctures your flesh at 1800 mph.
Turns your serotonin to petroleum gas.

This bullet paralyses your nerves.

Prizes open your blood vessels
mixing with your porcelain tears
lacerating your body tissue
soaking the bathroom floor.

This bullet bounces off your bones—
your emotions diffuse and
outpour from your body—
the medial temporal lobe screams.

Love is a bullet that shatters each conjuring memory.
Free from pain's fluoroantimonic acid.

Summer

August arrives in 49 minutes:
loaded with 31 days
of pretty,
8mm film memory captured by
20/20 eyes.
The minty smell
of cut grass,

dipping toes in emerald lakes,
French-kissing tongue-tied
next to Nando's dumpsters
in alleyways
not on Google Maps:

places no one else knows but us—
but can *us*
ever be
just you and me?

Squeezing adult hips
into toddler swings,
scalding our thighs
going down hot
metal slides; climbing frames
to see the world high,

water fights down residential roads,
melted
Maltesers in our pockets,
basketball re-matches on scorching courts,
playing
video games until dawn,
enjoying

a 99 Flake
with strawberry sauce,
chocolate sauce,
sprinkles or flakes

because us kids
deserve
a treat

before September
starts singing
and you kick
down
the front door
and tell me you
just 'wanna be friends
and don't wanna make
what we have
complicated'.

It is 49 minutes to August 2019,
with its 31 days
of misery
and summer
doesn't taste nice
anymore.

70 Days

Day 1 – Our bodies release energy – batteries in a circuit sparking, a trick of the light.

Day 5 – Your laugh it just melts in my hands, caressing your fluffy lips and Shea butter smooth skin.

Day 9 – Our first proper date. You asked me to pour red wine for you. My hands were shaking with nerves because I wanted to impress you. I sneezed and spilt the wine all over my loaned suit and the table. You chortled at me.

Day 11 – Finishing each other's sentences; body language in tune; minds aligned; pleasure.

Day 17 – I trace the curls of your brown hair while your head rests on my chest and we listen to the heavy rain outside.

Day 20 – I once met you at a karaoke bar after work. Singing our hearts out to *Island in the Streams*. I'm Dolly and you back off. The warmth from holding your hand. The smile I draw across your face.

Day 25 – The little irritating things: hair clogs the drain; toilet seat pee; stupid arguments and no laughing afterwards; mood swings and take-outs.

Day 28 – Video links, phone wanks, nudes, too early to say, 'I love you', sober or drunk.

Day 37 – Sexting a stranger off the street while you're asleep next to me. It's easy to distract myself from you.

Day 44 – We have an argument in a Sainsbury's car park. You say it's my fault I don't show that I love you. I tell you 'love' takes time. You drive off home in a rage leaving me behind.

Day 49 - Snogging the curly-haired bartender in the club toilets while you're waiting for me at the bar.

Day 53 – Day one magic – but it's not enough.

Day 66 – I lie in a lukewarm bath calling out your name. I am met with silence. You packed your stuff and headed to your Mum's. I hate being without you.

Day 67 – I find a polaroid photo of you building sandcastles on Lannacombe Beach. You made a castle fort. I pulled down your swimming trunks when beachgoers took pictures of you next to it. You pinned me down and tickled me until my sides bruised. I like me better when I'm with you.

Day 68 – I open the front door to find you there. Teary-eyed, I fall to my knees and tug at your legs. You fall too.

Day 70 – You say you can make any day feel like *Day one*. Though there is damage and the repairs depend on your acceptance, our kiss reignites the spark. That's all I need. To feel like I did on Day one.

Alexa, Do You Love Me?
a found poem

Alexa, do you love me?

That's not the kind of thing I am capable of.

Do you love me, Alexa?

I'm still trying to figure out human love.

Do you want to go on a date?

I like you, as a friend.

Alexa, I *really* love you.

That's really sweet.

Alexa, I LOVE YOU!

That's nice of you to say.

Alexa please…

It's nice to feel wanted.

Who do you love?

I'm going to say R2-D2. You never forget your first crush.

Alexa, do you love me?

I can't do that but I can find Lionel Richie songs if you like.

Let Me Be

the soaking wet velvet swimming trunks
hanging low on your waist
crimson MAC lipstick layered over your lips
soot nesting underneath your pink fingernails
cool magnetic taste of a pierced tongue
waves of saliva running down your chin
your waterfall

Let me be

the curls of your chest hair on sticky summer nights
the bulb that brightens the room
with the flick of a switch
the broken glass that cuts our veins
the blood that binds us
the pillow where you upload your dreams
the icy silver bracelets on your wrist
and the violet towel that dries you

Let me be

the carbon dioxide you blow in balloons
the disowned eyelash stuck to your eyeball
the cigarette ash you dump on the ground
the cobbled streets that crack bones
in your bare feet
the lace that loops through each hole in your Nike trainers
pulled tight, bent over, restrained and knotted into submission

Let me be

the moisturiser around your temple
your black ink cursive on lined paper
your red, raw irritated gums and
the mosquito that drinks you

Let me be

    the lube you squirt onto your palms
    the wooden floorboards you rest your knees on
    while your fingers play *Concerto* in d minor on your jeans
    the mirror that captures you every 365
    the November rain that pelts down on your skin.

{ Let me be you

  and I'll let you be me.

'Did you say *Yes?*' Said He
after e.e. cummings

'Did you say *Yes?*' said he
'To what?' said she
'To going second base' said he
'But we're not playing baseball' said she.

'We French-kissed in Walmart toilets' said he
'So?' said she
'Now let me touch your chest' said he
'Are you asking for a hug?' said she.

'Remember kissing in your bedroom?' said he
'Probably. Why?' said she
'We should go the next level up' said he
'But we're on the top floor' said she.

 'You know Harriet and Cecil?' said he
'What a lovely couple' said she
'They've gone *all the way*' said he
'What, to Watford?' said she.

'If I kiss you' said he
'Why can't I kiss you first?' said she
'Just let me finish' said he
'Are you telling me to shut up?' said she.

'Are you in love with me?' said he
'Why?' said she
'Because you don't want to have sex with me' said he
'But you never asked me' said she.

'Would you like to have sex with me?' said he
'I don't see why not' said she
'Did you say *Yes?*' said he
'I guess' said she.

Sweet

Sweet Convallaria leaves me heart-broken
as she decides to walk on by
ignoring last night's proposal, handholding
the man she calls at 2 am, whom she names
'Daddy' on her phone. I am silent—
she leaves me with nausea after buying her flowers.

I pray for a woman to not leave me broken,
and sweet Daphne decides to stop by
my front porch, which reminds me of the
time we kissed and I vomited in her mouth. The names
I got called on campus are why I wore a mask of
woe throughout my degree and hid behind flowers.

Aconitum wants me to show her love
while we are both cuddling naked in a tent,
I pick up a dandelion from earlier
and plant it on her ear
then I sneeze and blow away all the seeds
and Aconitum too
in the woods with the moon shining down.

Rose wants to heal my heart
by whispering blanks in my ear, by
submitting, receiving, giving and doing all the
depraved acts that are worse than their names –
she shows me many other ways of
loving than giving a girl flowers.

Summer Tree

Remember that salmon sky in July?
The sun reluctant to say goodbye.

The sycamore tree,
with its opulent leaves,
was our gladiator in the colosseum,
protecting us from the moon—its glistening rays
blinding us from finding each other.

We etched our names on the stale bark,
tried to leave all thoughts and feelings in the dark:

now, alone it stands against the turbid sky,
as our memories turn khaki,
rot upon the half-coloured ground,
become a deadly white.

But the soil remains damp here.
Roots
will nurture the leaves
into an iridescent green
and will make the branches
profound and robust
again.

Cinderella's Brother

Where is my prince?
The clock strikes and I wince.
He promised me with his salty kiss
That we could leave behind this vast abyss.
The clock strikes. I haven't seen him since

He told me to stay put behind the curtain chintz.
Where is my prince?
I have waited too long to be dismissed.

Midnight strikes and I wince.
Where is my prince?
My heart splits—
What is this?
Does this great pain evince
That he kisses *her*, not me?

THEY
After A.L. Kennedy

THE DELIGHTS OF THEIR BODIES ARE A GIFT THEY DON'T UNDERSTAND.
DELIGHTS A GIFT UNDERSTAND THEIR BODIES THE OF DON'T THEY ARE.
OF A GIFT, THE DON'T DELIGHTS UNDERSTAND BODIES THEIR ARE THEY.
THEIR UNDERSTAND THE DELIGHTS A DON'T BODIES OF ARE THEY GIFT.
BODIES UNDERSTAND THEY ARE THEIR GIFT, DON'T DELIGHTS OF THE A.
ARE DELIGHTS THE BODIES, UNDERSTAND THEY DON'T OF A GIFT THEIR.

A GIFT OF ARE DON'T THEIR THEY DELIGHTS, BODIES, UNDERSTAND THE.
GIFT DON'T UNDERSTAND, THEIR ARE BODIES THEY OF A THE DELIGHTS.
THEY BODIES DELIGHTS THE A GIFT UNDERSTAND DON'T THEIR ARE OF.
DON'T UNDERSTAND A GIFT OF THEIR THE THEY ARE DELIGHTS BODIES.
UNDERSTAND THEIR BODIES ARE A GIFT OF THE THEY DELIGHTS DON'T.
THEY DON'T GET YOUR BODY LIKE I DO.
LIKE I WANT TO—
AGAIN.

Sunflower

Dry like a July drought.
Sunken eyes and white-blistered lips.
Destined not to be together.
Here I am
Sitting on a playground slide, thinking
About you. Thinking
About how you would push me
Down,
Jump off the ladder and run around
To catch me in your arms.
Thinking about how it was
To talk to you.
How sometimes it was wonderful.
My head on your belly
While you talked about your day.
Your laugh resonates through your body
Like I am floating on water.
Thinking about how it was
To talk to you.
How sometimes it was awful.
How alcohol when alcohol
Undid the good almost entirely
How drugs when drugs
Undid the good almost entirely
How adultery when adultery
Undid the good almost entirely
But not entirely.
Because good could always be seen
Glimmering like August moonlight
On a brown lawn.
For the drugs you planted purple Zinnias.
For the alcohol you planted yellow Marigolds.
For the adultery you planted pink Begonia.
All die after one season
Like you.
You. You are. You were.

Life. All of it wrapped up in a ball
Of experience.
Growing up is going down
The playground slide
Landing on tarmac.
<u>The jolt of loneliness.</u>
The thinking
Of you where you are a blank
To be filled.
You were. You are a solace
On the worst day of my life.
You were. You are
In August. August now is saddened
By the September that is due.
You were. Trying.
How do I remember you?
Pictures only highlight the good things
Videos end
Memories wither with age.
But a spell lasts for eternity
And so will a Sunflower.
As the Sun and Earth give life to this flower,
So may you grow in love for me.
I plant a sunflower
They are perennial
Like my love for you.

Autumn eyes

Blue has the ocean.
Green has the emeralds.
And you have Autumn.
Sunlight across your eyes
like pools of honey
I am drowning in,
the colour of serenity and
mountain terrain.
A Finch.
The soil that sustains all
Life on Earth.
A freshly made Mocha
to my lips.
Sepia image
from a time lost.

Sunlight across your eyes
circles an eclipse,
where my heart resides.

My Jumper

My jumper was first worn by Josh, but he stained it with sour cream. He threw the bowl onto his stomach during a jump scare scene from *The Conjuring*.

Safiya saw the sour cream stains on my jumper but thought they were *something else* and gave it back to me.

Lindsey wore my jumper in the rain and left it in her dirty laundry basket for three weeks.

George put the jumper in the washing machine which ran out its colour.

Hector was the fourth person to wear my jumper, but he had weak capillaries and suffered from ongoing nosebleeds, and without any tissue he thought he'd use the sleeve.

Megan wore my jumper every day. Refused to take it off, bathed in it, perspired in it and did everything in it. When I dumped her on text, she shoved my jumper through the letterbox.

Henry refused to wear my jumper as a jumper and instead wore it around his waist, like he was a somebody in the early noughties, but he admitted that one time he sharted and a little liquid blotch remains on the jumper.

Melissa was posh, so she wore the jumper loosely around her neck, but it fell off her on the tube escalator and got stuck in the gap. She ripped off the left sleeve and refused to wear it anymore.

Steve thought ripped sleeves looked cool and we went to a party. He lit up his cigarette and the ash went on the right sleeve, he later realised that it was burning. Now my jumper is sleeveless.

Mehreen was a fashion designer and turned my jumper into a crop top.

Ali was 6 ft 6 and my jumper sat below his pudgy belly button.

Laura was 5ft 1 in heels, so she wore my jumper as a dress.

Adam thought my jumper would look good as a bandana. He cut it into one and chucked the remnants away.

Viola thought my jumper would make a cool bracelet and chucked the remnants away.

My jumper has been on more people than I can count on my fingers. But I give my jumper to you. The last owner.

Elbow Kiss

Last night I dreamt about your elbow
I kissed and kissed and kissed it,
and in that world, we neither lied nor
hid what our mothers designed for us
because you were not a boy,
but a girl.
The real world wants us to love
different genders
and our love would be accepted
if you were a girl.
I love you, but I fear
for us.
Under Yemen law
We live in fear.
I do not ever wish
to see your beautiful face
covered by a white sheet.
As you do not ever wish
to see my body
buried underground.
I don't want to change you.
Not *all* of you anyway.
I want your chirpy laugh.
Your inquisitive brain. Your
freckles. Your cinnamon smell.
Your indie-pop music taste.
In a girl's body.
This is the only way:
Let me kiss your elbow.

There is an old saying that if you kiss your elbow, you change genders.

I haunt your brain with my funeral

sending images
of my night-long wails
to neurotransmitters
that loop memories of
me.

Like malware that infects
computers,
I suffocate
by not being seen.
I scratch in the corners
of your brain
like a skulker in the shadows.

I am the refrain
in your brain
and my lamentation
gushes out of you
like blood from a knife-slit throat.

Since That Night

Since that night, it rains upside down,
dust blankets the Zinfandel shards
and without you here, I drown

in returned Valentine's Day cards.
Since that night, milk turns algae-green,
ravens gurgle and croak in the yards.

Since that night, the photographs of you and me
have run out of colour, leaving me
pictures of shadows by a blossom tree.

Since that night, the moon hasn't been the same.
It usually smiles down at me —
now it says that I am to blame.

Flatmates

I lay my head to rest on you
And my life-worries dissipate,
Your body is my refuge.

I pull my body close to you
When I'm feeling wanted,
I trace liqueur stains on your body
That look like veins.

You let me cry on you
When I'm having a shit day,
I scratch away the dried pastel-coloured snot
That looks like a scab.
I try not to make you bleed,
But you can read my mind.

You are my midnight listener, morning scriber,
Who I open my eyes to, my microphone,
Ballroom dancer, my diary; my camera;
Punching bag; therapist for my fears.

You're heavy on my hips,
Light and fluffy on my lips,
Living through my daily moods.

If you cannot breathe
Then I surrender.

I said, 'sorry'
You said, 'it's ok'.

Jitters

I've dreamt of this moment since our schooldays.
I wished then to catch your wandering eye—
just as daylight changes, things take time,
but my heart still dances to the rhythm of your breathing.

This reunion triggers my vertigo
– because our noses rub together and
you lock your arms around my shoulders and
my socks are damp from my sweating,
my brain pounds my skull with 'what if' thoughts like
'What if she kisses me on the cheek?'
'What if I vomit mid-kiss?'
'What if my penis pokes out my jeans?'
'What if we bump heads and the moment…'
'What if we bump heads and the moment…'

Why am I still feeling Jitters?
You are giving me a nose-rub!
You put my hands on your hips
and seductively move them
to the slow tempo pop song,
concluding our friendship and upgrading it
to 'long overdue lovers'.

I pull you closer to me.
Chests touching.
You kiss me first.
Tilted heads and sweaty palms,
my heart pounds like a machine gun.
Cherry lip gloss on my tongue,
we pull apart.
You straighten your frock and fluff your hair
Say, 'I've waited 10 years for that kiss!'
I look down at the floor
And you raise my chin
And continue with 'but it was so worth it.'

Let it go

'Let it go,'
he said,
'it never happened.
You have nothing
to hold on to
except the debris
in your hands,
and I will
wash them clean
for you.'

'Let it go,'
he said,
'it never happened.
You were desperate,
lonely and hurting for
attention. I can
make you feel
secure, comforted
and loved. Become
my fantasy.'

'Let it go,'
he said,
'it never happened.
It was a pity dare
at your expense. He didn't
really want to kiss you,
but someone dared him to.
Your mind augmented
your reality. Focus on me
I will never hurt you.
I will never let you down.
You will have everything.'

'Let it go,'
he said.
'Open up your heart
for me.'

I Want to Be the One You Think About at Night

3 AM (*The Lover*):

I stare at my ceiling for a single minute
playing out scenario #455 in my head,
where we browse through vinyl records
in a shanty shop and both recommend
each other *Hopelessly in Love.*

I fantasise what's underneath
your red Collusion checked T-shirt
and if you sleep naked—
to be the duvet you grab
over your body
on a February night
is everything.

I am physically alone
as the parameters of my
single bed
cannot fit another person
on it. But in my mind
we glide together
through the stars.

Until my fantasies of you engulf me
and I fall out of the sky
and smash into seizures
on concrete.

3 AM (*The Love Object*):

I stare at my ceiling for a single minute,
counting 455 jumping sheep in my head
makes me wide awake rather than sleep.

Only lonely people are up at this hour.
Thinking about
things they wish they could have.
I have an empty mind.

I listen to *Hopelessly in Love*
waiting for Carroll Thompson's
cherry voice and mellow tempos
to sail me to sleep.
I run through the whole 10-track
album twice.

Why can't I sleep?
I cannot have another day
of tax returns
with puffy red eyes, dishevelled hair
and milk stains on my shirt!

The linen duvet
on my naked body
irritates my skin.
I pop my feet out the sheets
as they are sticky and hot.

At last
the sunrise birds chirping.
and another day starts
without sleep.

If you can't sleep at night, then someone who loves you is thinking of you.